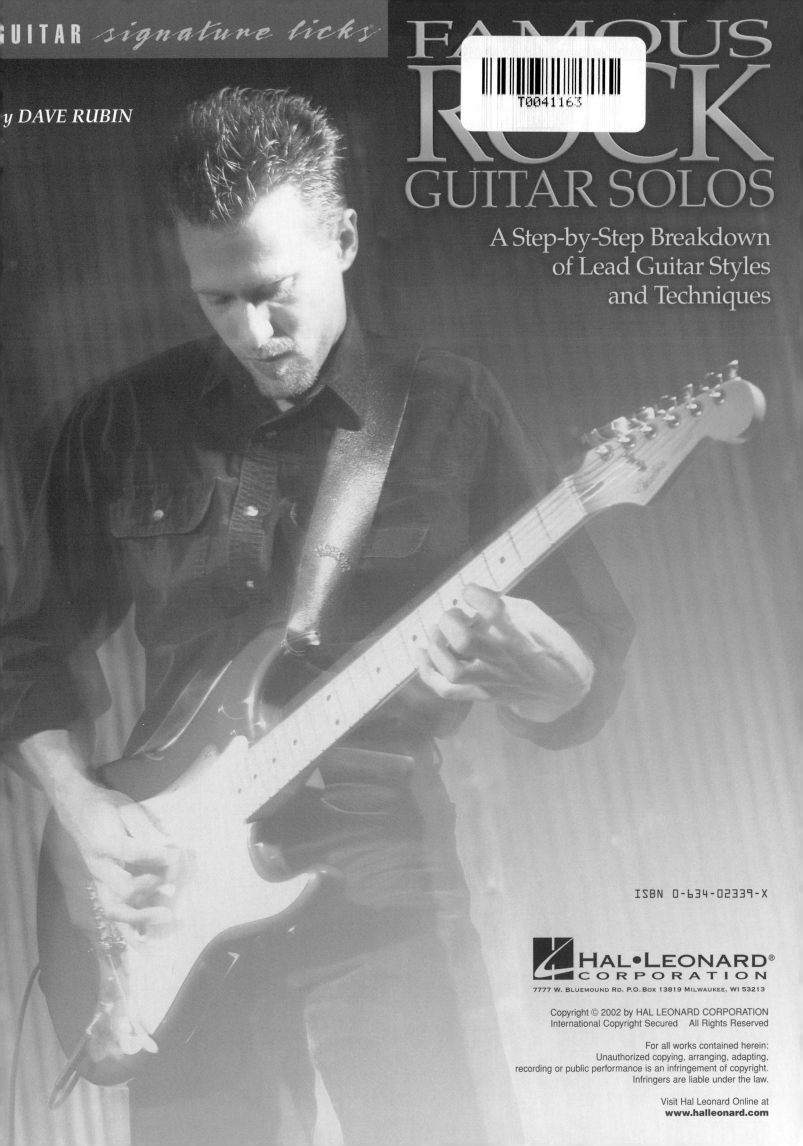

GUITAR *signature licks*

FAMOUS ROCK GUITAR SOLOS

by DAVE RUBIN

A Step-by-Step Breakdown
of Lead Guitar Styles
and Techniques

ISBN 0-634-02339-X

HAL•LEONARD®
CORPORATION

7777 W. BLUEMOUND RD. P.O. BOX 13819 MILWAUKEE, WI 53213

Visit Hal Leonard Online at
www.halleonard.com

—

CONTENTS

INTRODUCTION

For the better part of two decades, electric guitarists had to battle saxophone players for solo space. When Gibson produced the first commercially viable electric guitar in 1937—the ES-150—it was the culmination of a quest to amplify the instrument in order to be heard above the brass and rhythm section. The electric pioneers Charlie Christian and T-Bone Walker soon discovered, however, that the result was not just a *louder* guitar, but one with a thick, cutting tone that could compete with the saxophone in the improvisational arena. Though other blues and jazz masters like brothers Johnny and Oscar Moore, Carl Hogan, Barney Kessel, and Bill Jennings would prove to *guitarists* in the forties the potential for the new electronic invention, it would take until the dawning of rock 'n' roll for the audience to catch up. Teenagers responded when Bill Haley and His Comets, with the legendary virtuoso Danny Cedrone on lead guitar, shocked the staid record industry with the success of "Rock Around the Clock" in 1954. A year later in Memphis, Elvis exposed the "dangerous" combination of a good-looking white guy promoting sex and R&B to rebellious teens. His version of Little Junior Parker's "Mystery Train" featured Scotty Moore picking a hybrid of country and blues guitar in a momentous creation that came to be called rockabilly. With Chuck Berry also leading the way at the same time in Chicago, clanging double-stops "like ringing a bell" and "duckwalking" to beat the band, it would only be a matter of time before the "honkers" would be directed to playing jazz, R&B, and eventually soul music as the amplified guitar took root.

That time arrived in early 1964, when the Beatles played on the *Ed Sullivan Show* in a landmark performance echoing Presley's epochal appearance eight years earlier. Though the Beatles were more like a top vocal group with accompaniment, the rhythm guitar interplay between John Lennon and George Harrison was as telepathic as had been between Muddy Waters and Jimmy Rogers ten years earlier in the blues, *and* their guitars were recorded prominently in the mix. When he did solo, Harrison usually played in the style of his hero Carl Perkins. In 1970, however, he peeled off a raw, raunchy bluesy solo on "Let It Be" more in the manner of his buddy Eric Clapton. Ole' "Slowhand" himself had previously (in 1968) turned in a scalding wah-wah solo with Cream on "White Room" at the height of the blues-rock era. Carlos Santana, one of the featured guitarists at Woodstock—the central event of the late sixties in 1969—was a standout among a bumper crop of hair-raising axemen on the scene. By the release of his second album, *Abraxas*, in 1970, his instrumental virtuosity was being acknowledged on Latin rockers like Tito Puente's "Oye Como Va."

Though the seventies lacked the seemingly boundless creativity of the sixties, there was no shortage of guitar power. From across the deep Atlantic, Deep Purple unleashed a rock classic in 1972 with "Smoke on the Water" sporting Richie Blackmore's immortal "music-store" hook. Stateside, Gary Richrath and REO Speedwagon from the Midwest were one of the pioneers of "arena rock" with the title track "Ridin' the Storm Out" from their third album in 1973. Rick Derringer, having been a teenage star with the McCoys in the mid-sixties and a sideman for Johnny Winter, struck out on his own and waxed a classic version of his "Rock and Roll Hoochie Koo" in 1974. Concurrently, the South was rising again—at least musically. The Allman Brothers had a big hit in 1973 thanks to Dickey Betts' exuberant "Ramblin' Man." Their fellow "rebels" Lynyrd Skynyrd waved the flag high for Southern rock with their second release in 1974, containing J.J. Cales' boogie blues of "Call Me the Breeze" as driven hard by Gary Rossington. A third stylistic departure of the "smiley-face" decade arrived in the form of glam rock, spearheaded by the outrageous Kiss and Ace Frehley, who slayed with the live, anthemic "Rock and Roll All Nite" in 1975. Lead singer Steven Tyler of Aerosmith had "eyes" for the same glam spotlight, but it was the heavy blues-rock leanings of Joe Perry that helped propel tunes like "Sweet Emotion" the same year.

Punk rock in the late seventies eschewed "pretentious" and "self-indulgent" improvisation for a quick three-chord bash, but heavy metal provided the antidote in the eighties. Judas Priest also played loud and fast like the punkers, but K.K. Downing and Glen Tipton riffed and soloed unashamedly, and the band had a certifiable hit with "Living After Midnight" in 1980. By this point, pop rock had discovered the appeal of big guitars (and big hair on the gents), and Pat Benatar's "Hit Me with Your Best Shot" hit the charts with assistance from producer Neil Geraldo's Van Halen-influenced solo.

After a fallow period in the seventies, blues was brought to the fore in the eighties by soul man Robert Cray and especially Texan Stevie Ray Vaughan. "Pride and Joy" from 1982 showed the viability of the shuffle beat, and Stevie's unabashed virtuosity has spawned a never-ending stream of imitators. Speaking of the blues, guitar god Eric Clapton continued his on-again, off-again love affair with the genre on record by releasing the hard-rocking *Journeyman* in 1989 containing the melodic "Pretending." Second-generation white blueser Kenny Wayne Shepherd, hungry to wear the mantle left behind by SRV, kicked up quite a fuss in the nineties and scored a hit in 1998 with the brooding "Blue on Black." The once-popular first cousin to the blues, swing music, had a (too) brief revival in the late nineties. Brian Setzer, the extraordinary guitarist from the neo-rockabilly Stray Cats, made jumping, jiving, and wailing on the guitar hip again with his sensational cover of Louis Prima's "Jump, Jive an' Wail" in 1998.

Famous Rock Guitar Solos is a delirious and delicious potpourri of fret-bending, string-torturing, high-flying hijinks guaranteed to drive guitarists to their instruments. Plug in, turn on, and crank it up while imagining your sound filling the hall to screaming adulation.

BLUE ON BLACK
(KENNY WAYNE SHEPHERD)

Words and Music by Tia Sillers, Mark Selby and Kenny Wayne Shepherd

Born in Shreevesport, Louisiana on June 12, 1977, Kenny Wayne Shepherd was taken at the age of seven by his father to see Stevie Ray Vaughan in concert, and the effect was life-changing. Shortly thereafter, Kenny began learning licks off of his father's extensive blues record collection, and by 13 he was good enough to sit in with local pros like Bryan Lee. After forming a band with lead singer Corey Sterling (since replaced by Noah Hunt), a deal with Giant Records was negotiated in 1993, and *Ledbetter Heights* arrived in 1995 to great acclaim, selling a phenomenal 500,000 copies by 1996. His second album, *Trouble Is...*, scored a Grammy nomination in 1998.

Figure 1

The sixteen-measure solo consists of the two-measure vamp of Rhy. Fig. 1 (D5–Csus2–D5–Csus2–D5 and Cadd9–G/B–G) played six times. Four measures of F–G–F–G complete the section. Shepherd (Gtr. 2) squeezes squealing blues licks from the root and extension positions of the D minor pentatonic scale. In measure 11 he builds intensity and a semi-climax with a series of bends to A in the "Albert King box" that resolve to the root (D) of the key, followed by a bluesy run down the root position of the D scale in measure 12 that likewise resolves briefly to string 6 (D) open.

Shepherd sets the stage for his finale by clicking on the 5th (C) and emphasizing the root (F) in measure 13 and anticipating the next chord (G) by tattooing the root on beat 4. Revving up, he honks down on F/C (root and 5th) while hammering from the 2nd (G) to the major 3rd (A), transposing this move up a step for the following G chord.

Fig. 1

Gtrs. 2 & 3: Drop D tuning:
(low to high) D–A–D–G–B–E

Guitar Solo
Moderately slow ♩ = 78

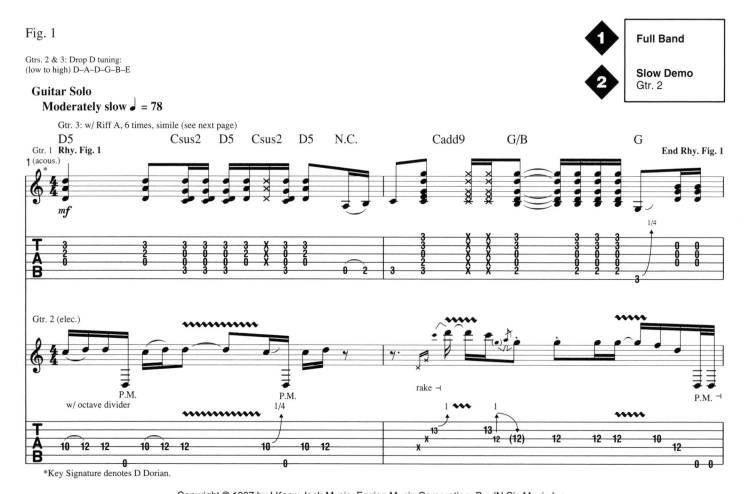

*Key Signature denotes D Dorian.

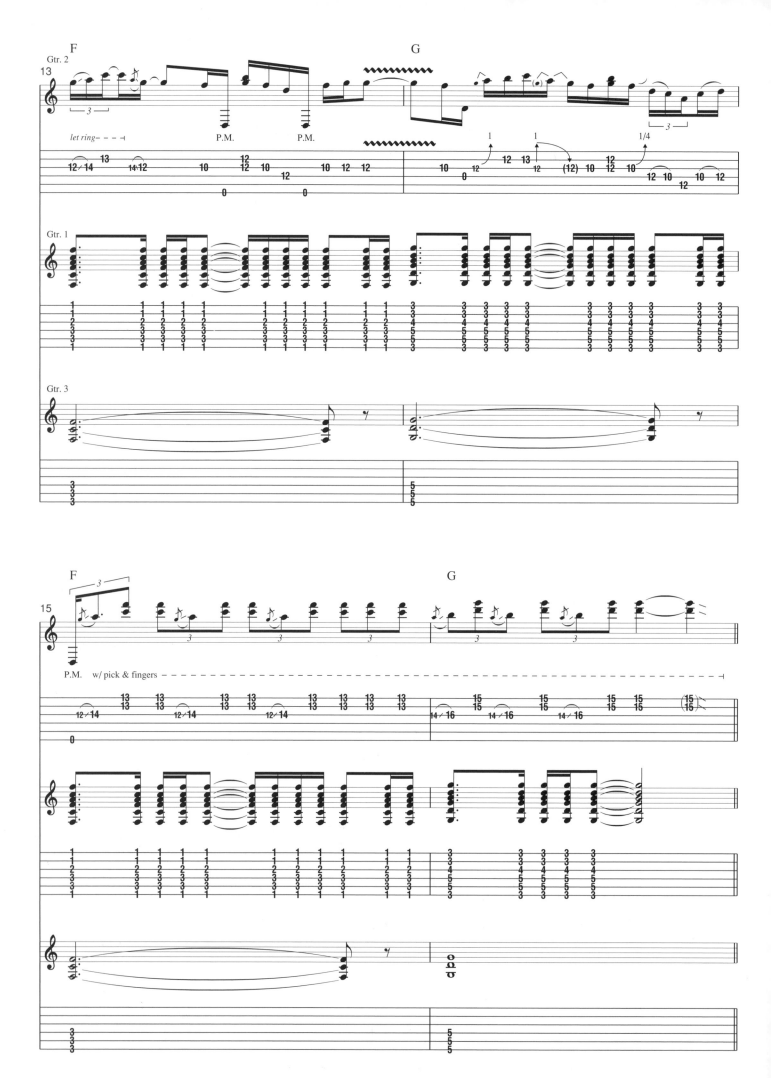

CALL ME THE BREEZE
(LYNYRD SKYNYRD)
Words and Music by John Cale

Lynyrd Skynyrd's 1973 debut album, *Pronounced Leh-Nerd Skin-Nerd*, flew in the face of convention with "Freebird," an epic guitar orgy, as the centerpiece. Along with opening for the Who on their *Quadrophenia* tour, it provided the Skynyrds with a measure of success that carried over to their sophomore effort, *Second Helping*, in 1974.

"Call Me the Breeze" is a 24-measure boogie blues. The solo finds Gary Rossington running roughshod through two choruses with his Les Paul barking like a hound running after a rabbit.

Figure 2

Rossington (Gtr. 3) throws down the gauntlet right quick in measures 1–8 (I) with the classic Robert Johnson/Muddy Waters triple-stop consisting of C♯/G/E (3rd/♭7th/5th). From there on through to measure 48, Rossington manipulates the A composite blues scale (A–B–C–C♯–D–D♯–E–F♯–G) to chart the changes. Some highlights:

Measures 13-16 (I): With E/C (5th and ♭3rd) bent a hip quarter step, followed by the root (A) and ♭7th (G), a repeating lick that implies the tonality with a decidedly blues dissonance creates texture.

Measures 17-21 (V, IV, and I): By repeating an eighth-note lick of D, C, E, and G over the three changes, tension and forward motion is conjured that releases to...

Measures 22-24 (I): ...a climb up the fingerboard from the fifth to the twelfth position where...

Measures 25-32 (I): ...the 2nd (B) is bent one step to the 3rd (C♯) and alternated with the 5th (E) to form a dyad of a 3rd (E/C♯) that implies A major.

Measures 43 and 44 (IV): The 5th (A) is played on string 1 while the root (D) is bent one step to the cool 9th (E) on string 3 for an extended harmony.

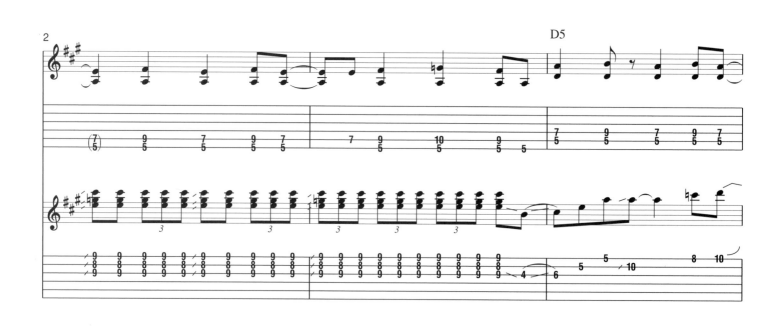

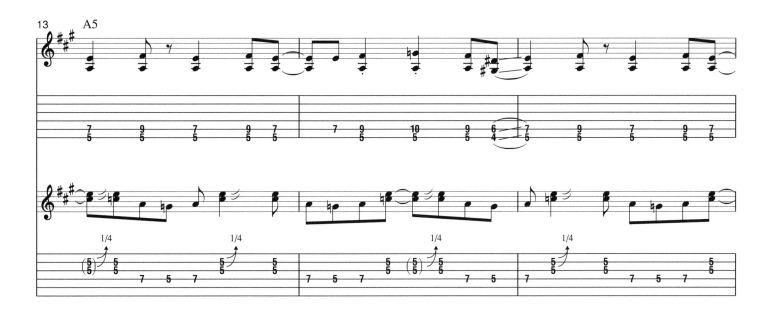

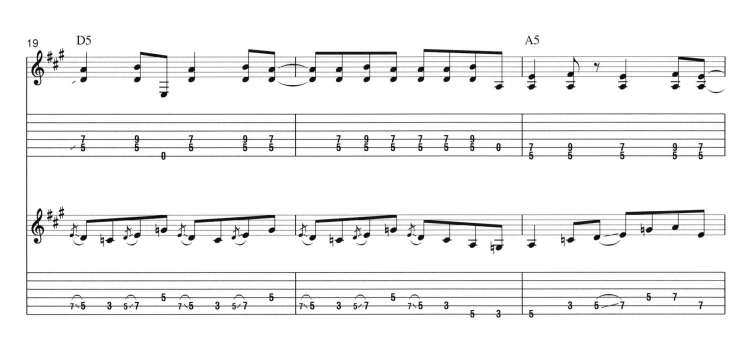

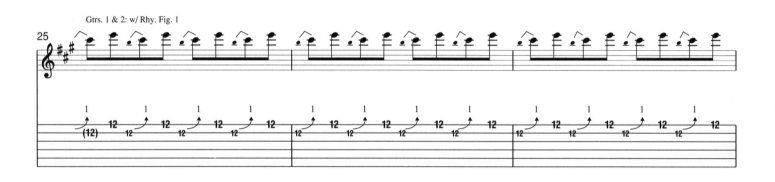

Gtrs. 1 & 2: w/ Rhy. Fig. 1

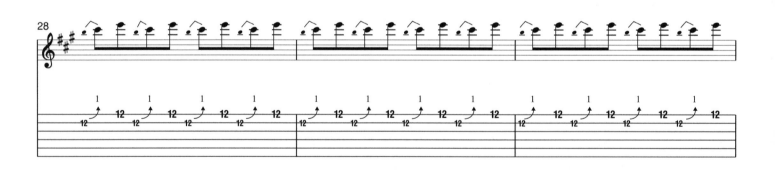

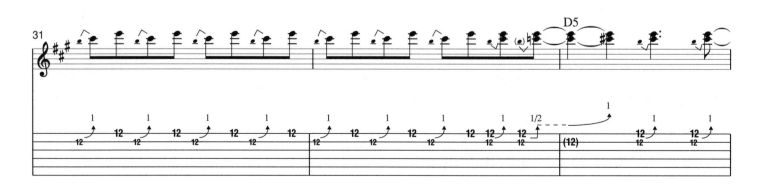

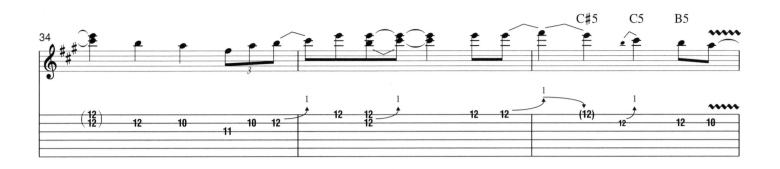

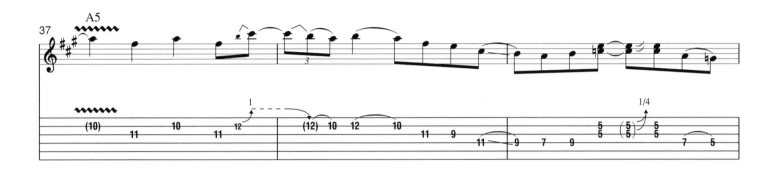

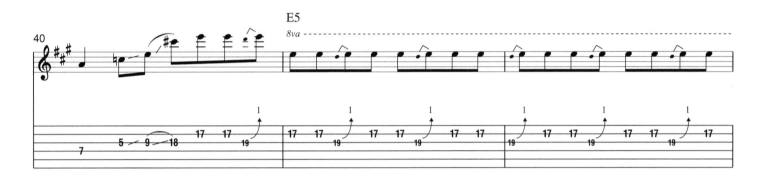

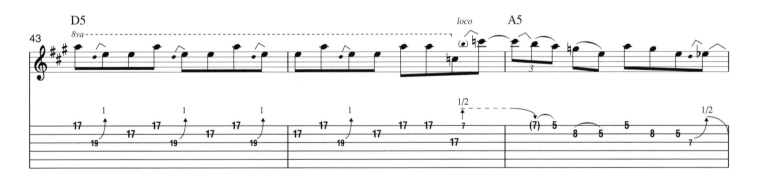

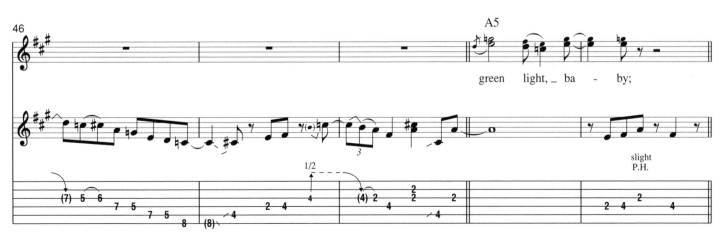

green light, _ ba - by;

HIT ME WITH YOUR BEST SHOT

(PAT BENATAR)

Words and Music by Eddie Schwartz

Born Pat Andrzejewski in Brooklyn, New York on January 10, 1953, Pat Benatar was one of the female groundbreakers in the eighties. Benatar was discovered in New York City at the Catch a Rising Star club in 1979 and signed a deal with Chrysalis Records. *In the Heat of Night* was quickly released, followed by *Crimes of Passion* in 1980 containing the #9 charting "Hit Me with Your Best Shot."

Figure 3

Pat's hubby Neil Geraldo "fires away" over the verse and chorus chords for a muscular, melodic sixteen-measure solo that careens between registers for impressive dynamics. In measure 1 he assails the root octave position with the 3rd (G#), 5th (B), major 7th (D#), and root (E) notes over the I chord and the B and C# notes over the V and vi changes to establish the overall tonality.

In measures 5 and 6 he contrasts "slower," syncopated eighth notes against the slippery sixteenth-note licks in the previous measures. Playing with the dynamics for good effect, Geraldo bends the 2nd (C#) of B up to the 3rd and sustains it before resolving to the root (B) in measure 8.

The next four-measure section (measures 1–4 of the chorus pattern) evolves to a new feel with F# and B creating pleasant tension through repetition in measures 9 and 10 while easily harmonizing (as in measures 5 and 6) over the chords. In measures 13–15 Geraldo wrenches down on a series of bends involving 5th (B) and root (E) notes as he figuratively slows the passage of time before climaxing with a pick-muted, staccato ascending run of B, C#, and D# that resolves to the root on beat 4 of measure 16.

| **5** | **Full Band** |
| **6** | **Slow Demo** Gtr. 3 |

Fig. 3

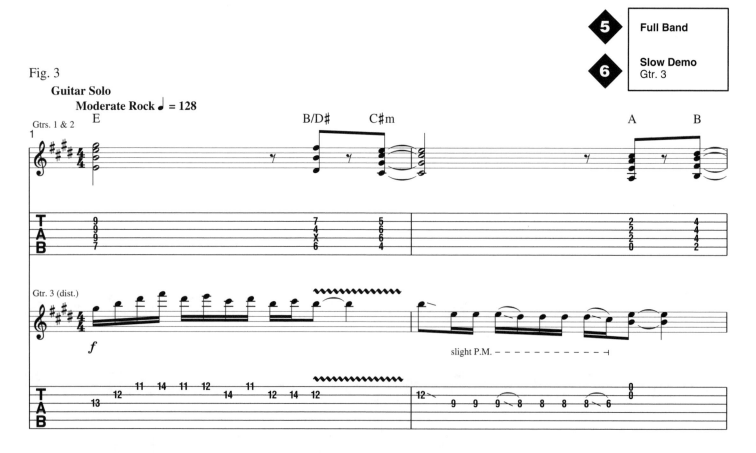

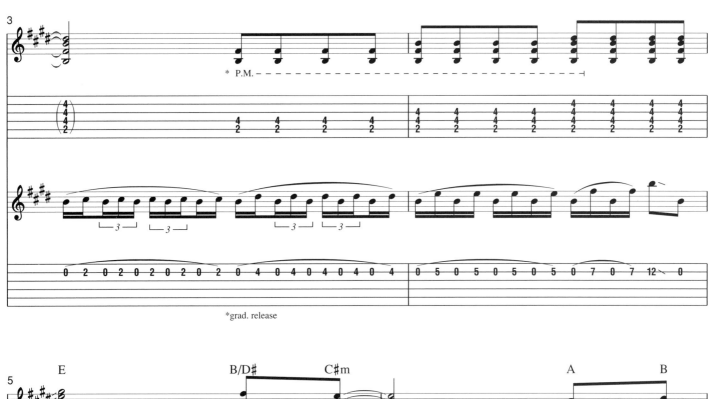

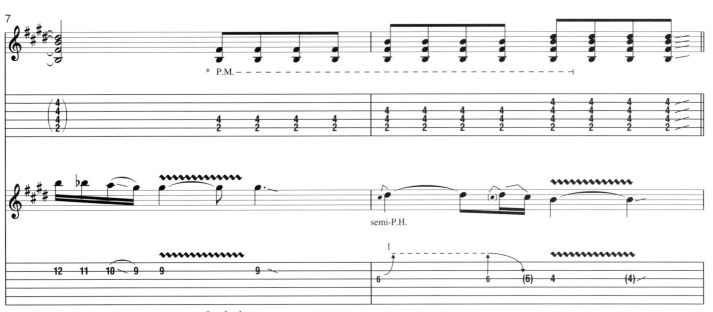

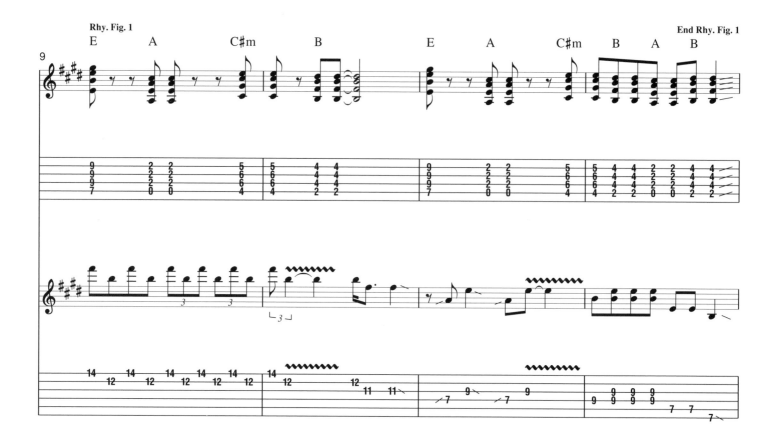

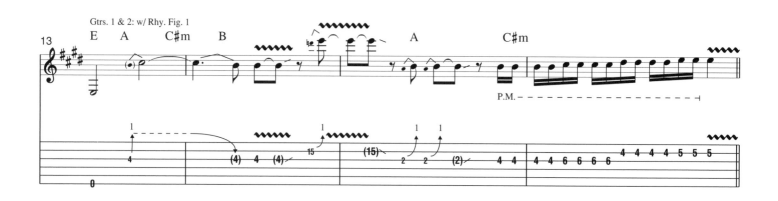

JUMP, JIVE AN' WAIL
(THE BRIAN SETZER ORCHESTRA)
Words and Music by Louis Prima

Brian Setzer was born on April 10, 1959 in Long Island City, New York. Between the ages of eight and eighteen he learned the guitar and the euphonium (!) and thought about leading a big band on guitar after seeing Mel Lewis at the Village Vanguard. Then he got kicked in the ear by punk in the mid-seventies and started a trio in 1978 with Slim Jim Phantom and Lee Rocker called the Bloodless Pharaohs. Seeing the wild audience reaction to the rockabilly classics that ended their sets, they changed musical direction and became the Tom Cats before settling on the Stray Cats.

"Jump, Jive an' Wail" was originally waxed by hep cat Louis Prima with Sam Butera honking on tenor sax, but Setzer turned it into a neo-swing guitar standard with his ultimate interpretation, as heard on the 1998 album *The Dirty Boogie*.

Figure 4

"Jump, Jive an' Wail" is an uptempo 12-bar blues with a fast, single chorus for the solo. Always thinking like a master trio guitarist, Setzer creates a dynamic "call-and-response" musical statement out of his solo with cool comp chords in measures 5, 7, and 11 (Bb7), and in measure 8 (Eb7), in contrast to the pull-offs. Adding to the effect is his relatively subtle application of the whammy bar to the Bb7 chords. In measures 14 and 15 (turnaround) he improvises in the root position of the Bb composite scale, with emphasis in measure 14 on the major 3rd (D) via a swooping, one-step bend from the 9th (C), along with the root (Bb), 6th (G), and 5th (F). In measure 15, Setzer draws on the blues for a typical bend of the 4th (Eb) to the 5th released and pulled off on the way to the root on beat 2. On beat 3 he also seems to be executing another cliché when he bends the b3rd (Db) a half step to the 3rd.

Performance Tip: Though a challenge, the most efficient and logical way to play the pull-offs is with the pinky, ring, and index fingers.

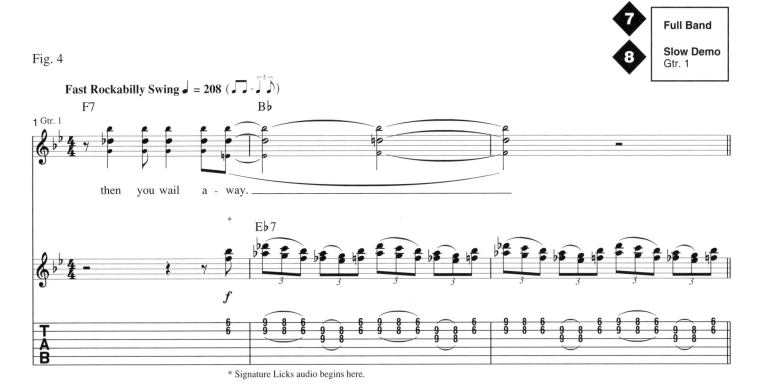

Fig. 4

* Signature Licks audio begins here.

LET IT BE
(THE BEATLES)
Words and Music by John Lennon and Paul McCartney

In the Beatles' canon, *Let It Be* closes out the Fab Four's ten-year odyssey through the sixties. Chronologically, however, most of it was recorded before *Abbey Road* in early 1969. The title track went to #1 (as did "The Long and Winding Road") and is actually one of the strongest tunes on the record, as well as a fine Paul McCartney composition. The George Harrison solo shown here is from the single, which differs from the *Let It Be* album version overdubbed later.

Figure 5

The solo is played over the eight-measure verse and is a textbook of how to employ the (A) relative (to C major) minor scale in several positions for maximum effect. Check out Harrison's fluttery, organ-like Leslied tone on the original recording. Some highlights:

Measure 3 (C and G): Harrison glides fluidly up through the root and extension positions of the scale with attention paid to the G (5th) and E (3rd) notes over the C chord, and the root (G), 6th (E), 5th (D), and sus4 (C) notes over the G.

Measure 5 (C and G): Harrison moves up from the third position with the D bent one step to the major tonality-defining 3rd (E) followed by the root (C). He then plays the 6th (A) and 5th (G) before he bends the D to E again in the root position of the A scale at fret 5. Over the G chord he emphasizes the 5th (D) and 2nd (A) notes.

Measure 6 (Am, Fmaj7, and F6): The E (5th) and G (♭7th) notes again serve to suggest the Am with the 5th (C) carrying the two F chords.

Measure 7 (C and G): Ascending for the first time to the upper strings in the extension position of the A scale at fret 8 for the climax, Harrison outlines and extends the harmony of the C chord with the root (C), 6th (A), 5th (G) and 3rd (E).

Measure 8 (F and C): Harrison slips in a fast gliss of A/E (major 7th and 3rd) to G/D (6th and 9th) before ending with the blues-approved string 3 lick of the D bent one step to the E.

Performance Tip: Use the ring and pinky fingers for the dyads in measure 8 so that the bend can be executed with the ring finger, then resolve to the C note with the vibratoing index finger.

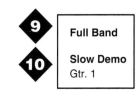

♦9   **Full Band**

♦10   **Slow Demo** Gtr. 1

Fig. 5

Ballad ♩ = 70

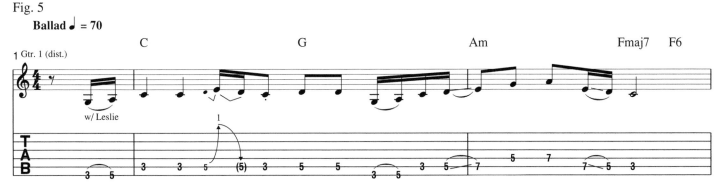

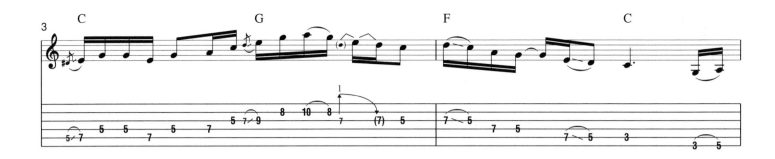

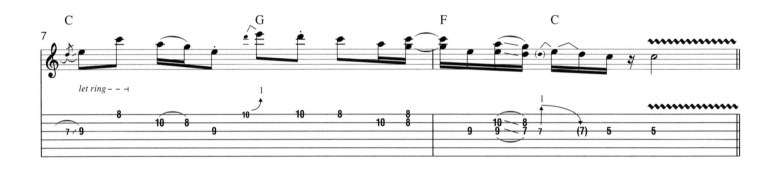

LIVING AFTER MIDNIGHT
(JUDAS PRIEST)
Words and Music by Glen Tipton, Rob Halford and K.K. Downing

Priest ruled at the start of the eighties, but speed/thrash metal groups like Metallica were breathing down their necks by mid-decade and making them sound quaint in comparison. Both the quality of their recordings and their popularity would wax and wane through to the early nineties, when lead singer Rob Halford began the thrash band Fight and then quit.

"Living After Midnight" and "Breaking the Law" were both hit singles from 1980's *British Steel*, a decidedly simpler, commercial venture from which Priest would eventually recoil aesthetically with *Ram It Down* in 1988. "Living After Midnight," vaguely reminiscent of early Deep Purple, contains a positively bluesy solo by the normally deranged K.K. Downing.

Figure 6

Over the hooky, anthemic, upbeat chords of the eight-measure chorus, Downing (Gtr. 3) slips comfortably into the octave root position of the E minor pentatonic scale and the root position of the C♯ relative minor (to E major) scale. Downing hunkers down modally, repeatedly returning to the root (E) in measures 1–6, often with sassy vibrato as in measures 2, 3, and 6. In measure 7 he tips his hand, however, leaping up to the twenty-second position where he bends the A (♭7th of B) one step up to B (root) followed by the D (♭3rd). He then reaches a climax by re-bending the A to B, releasing back to A and ending with the screaming bent B sustaining and warbling into measure 8.

Performance Tip: In measure 7, slide up to the D at fret 19 with the index finger, using the ring finger to bend the A to B at fret 22 and the pinky to access the high D on string 1.

Fig. 6

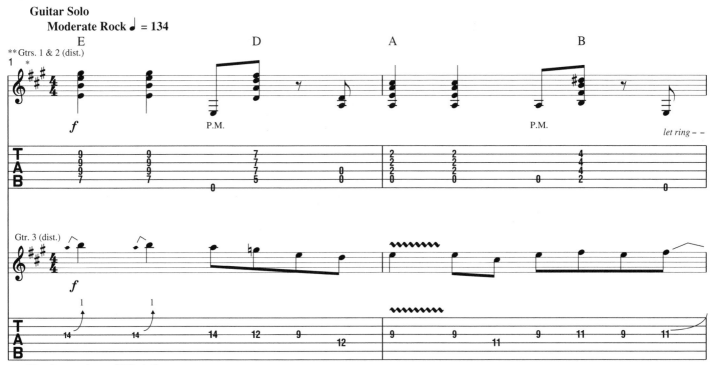

*Key signature denotes E Mixolydian.
**composite arrangement

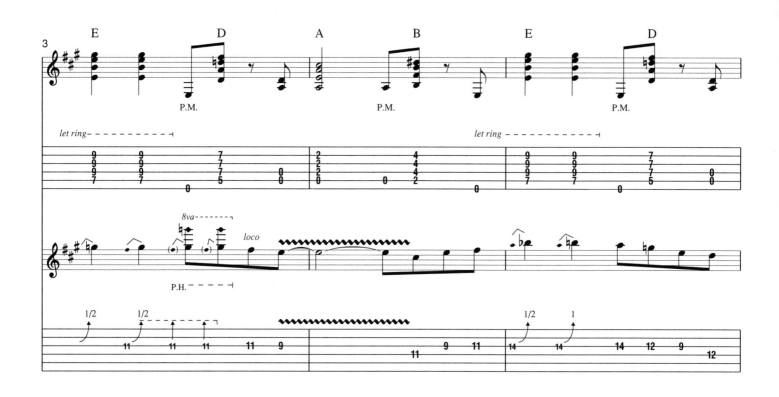

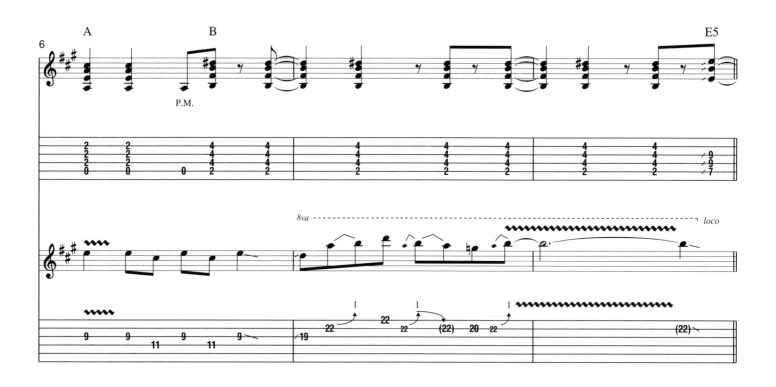

MYSTERY TRAIN
(ELVIS PRESLEY)
from ELVIS ON TOUR
Words and Music by Sam C. Phillips and Herman Parker, Jr.

"Mystery Train" was the R&B side of the 1955 single, with "I Forgot to Remember to Forget" the country side. It became Elvis' first #1 country hit, but the shock waves building across the country for him would soon compel RCA Records to buy his contract from Sam Phillips (for the then-princely sum of $35,000) and turn him into a pop star.

Figure 7

The sixteen-measure solo changes in "Mystery Train" are much more conventional than the abnormal twenty-eight-measure verses. The solo changes progress as follows: IV (A) = four measures, I (E) = four measures, V (B) = two measures, IV = two measures, and I = four measures. In measures 1–4 (IV), Scotty Moore alternates open-position A and A7 voicings in a manner similar to country-blues guitarists. For the V (B7) chord in measures 9 and 10, Moore relocates to fret 7 and chooses the root (B), 3rd (D♯), ♭7th (A), and 5th (F♯) notes from the B Mixolydian mode to imply a B7 tonality. In measures 11 and 12 (IV), he shifts down to the 5th position, but not before using the ♭7th of B at fret 10 as the root (A) of the IV chord in beat 1 of measure 11.

In measure 13, Moore repeats the one-measure I–IV "hook" from the intro and verse that has become one of the foundation riffs of rockabilly music.

Performance Tip: Though the notes in measures 5-12 are theoretically derived from the named scale, in reality Moore is locking his hand into a chord shape at each fret position and picking the individual notes.

Fig. 7

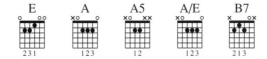

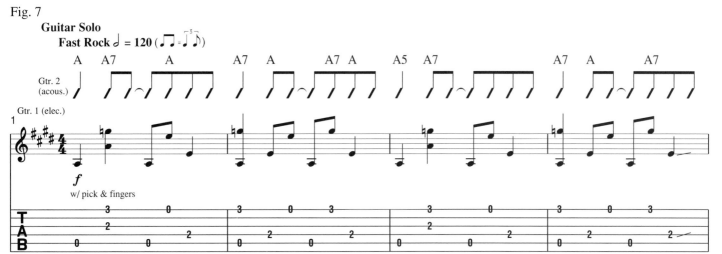

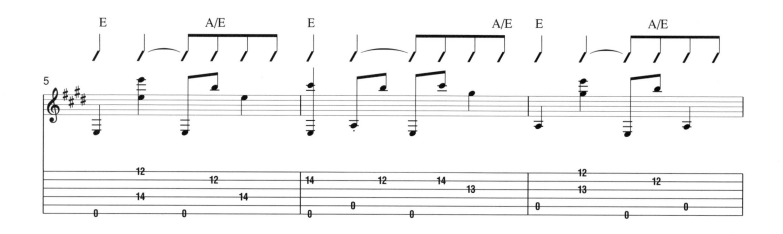

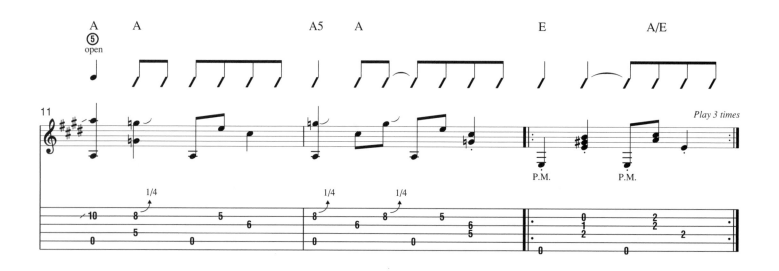

OYE COMO VA
(SANTANA)
Words and Music by Tito Puente

Carlos Santana was born July 20, 1947 in Autlan de Navarro, Mexico. He moved to San Francisco in the early sixties and formed the Santana Blues Band in 1966. A year later the name was shortened to Santana, and in 1968 the band signed with Columbia Records. In August 1969, their self-titled debut album was released, selling 2 million copies. The 1970 follow-up, *Abraxas*, sold 4 million copies and featured the hit covers of "Black Magic Woman" (by Peter Green) and "Oye Como Va" that reached #4 and #20, respectively.

Figure 8—Solo 1 and Interlude

Over a twenty-six-measure i–IV (Am7–D9) vamp (including a six-measure interlude), Santana plumbs the A Dorian mode in the root position with a sensuous touch. In measures 1 (i) and 2 (IV), he emphasizes the minor tonality-defining ♭3rd (C) and ♭7th leading tone (G) over Am7 and the root (D) over D9. In measure 14 (IV), Santana plays two hip dyads (F♯/D and E/C) that imply D major to D9 chords with thirds.

The interlude, which functions as a natural conclusion to the solo, features a two-measure motif consisting of the ♭3rd (C) repeated and emphasized over the Am7 chord and a bluesy bass line over the D9 that "walks" chromatically from F♯–G–G♯–A (3rd–4th–♯4th–5th).

15 Full Band

16 Slow Demo
Gtr. 2

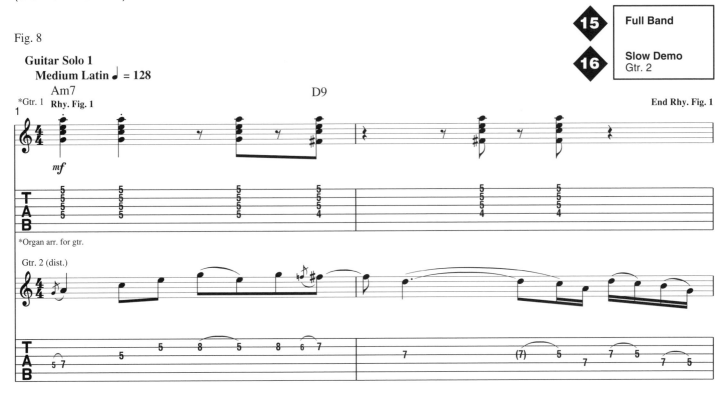

Fig. 8

Guitar Solo 1
Medium Latin ♩ = 128

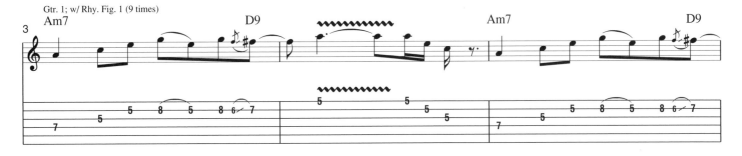

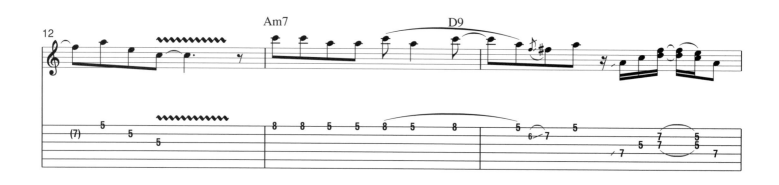

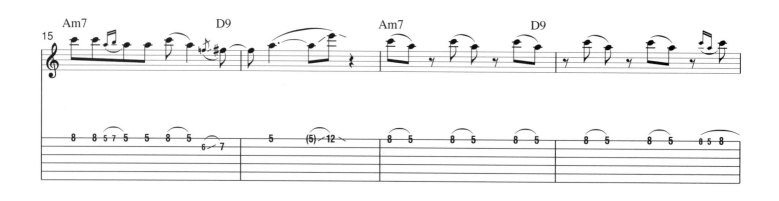

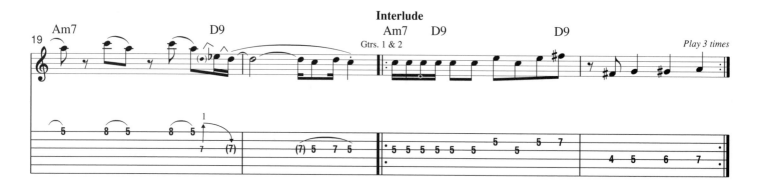

Figure 9—Solo 2

Starting in measure 9 (i), Santana relocates to the octave root position of the A Dorian mode at fret 17, bending and releasing the ♭7th (G) a full step for a flute-like effect. Picking up momentum, he drops back to the octave root position of the A Dorian mode at fret 5 in measures 11 and 12 and makes the "Chuck Berry (by way of T-Bone Walker) unison bend" sound fresh by applying vigorous vibrato at the peak of each bend. He goes out in measures 19–24 with the C (♭3rd of A, ♭7th of D) and A (root of A, 5th of D) notes.

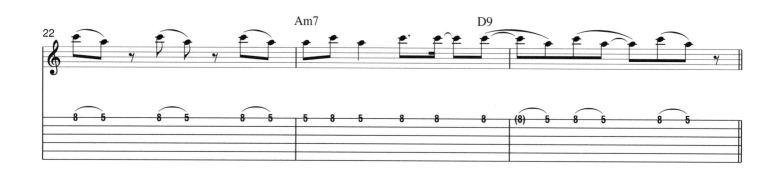

PRETENDING
(ERIC CLAPTON)
Words and music by Jerry Williams

That Eric Clapton (born March 30, 1945 in Ripley, Surrey, England) is one of the greatest electric guitarists of all time is beyond dispute. The real question is whether he is a bluesy rocker or a rocking bluesman. "Pretending" is the opening track on *Journeyman* from 1989. With guest shots by Robert Cray and the late George Harrison, as well as Phil Collins, Richard Tee, and Jim Keltner, it features strong songwriting and production values.

Figure 10—Solo 1

Clapton solos with a thick, swirling tone over the eight-measure verse of I (E), I, ♭III (G/E), ♭III, IV (A7), IV, I, and I. Over the IV chord in measures 5 and 6 he emphasizes the ♭7th (G) leading tone to help define the chord change. As measures 1–6 contain notes and bends designed to create musical tension, Clapton uses measures 7 and 8 to resolve heavily to the root via a half-step bend to the major 3rd (G♯) on string 3 and then winds the solo down by literally descending on string 6 down to the ♭3rd (G) with a tone in the lower register that gets "froggy" and vocal-like.

19 Full Band

20 Slow Demo
Gtr. 1

Fig. 10

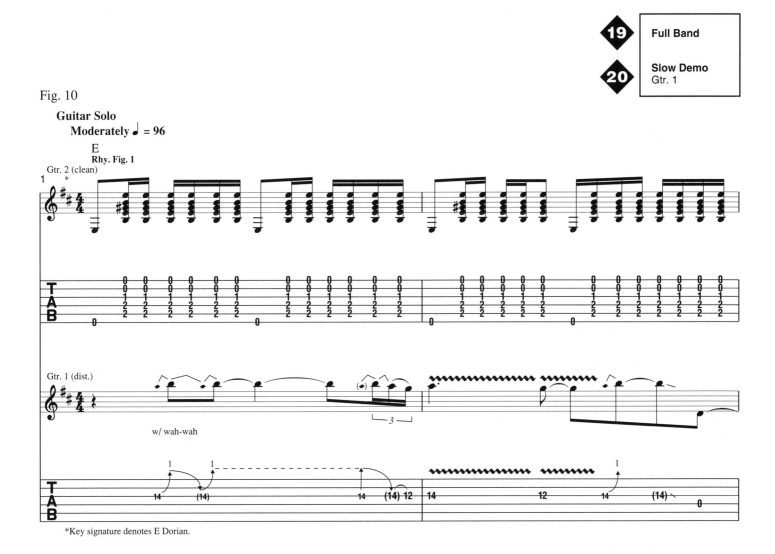

*Key signature denotes E Dorian.

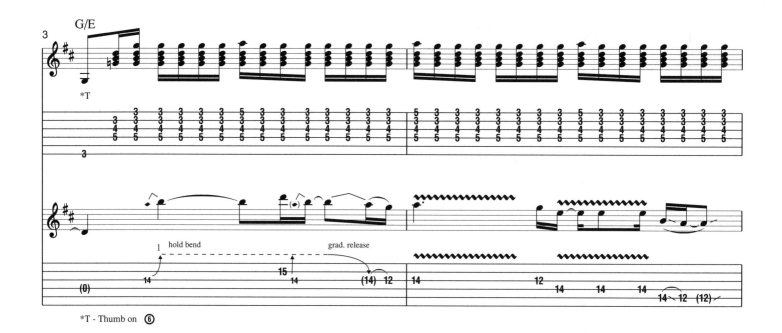

*T - Thumb on ⑥

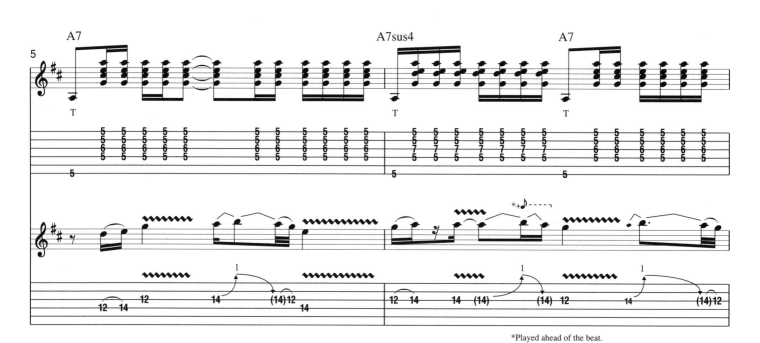

*Played ahead of the beat.

End Rhy. Fig. 1

Figure 11—Outro Solo

As the verse chords start the fade-out, Clapton barks out licks around the fifth position of the E minor pentatonic scale with phrasing and tone that is reminiscent of a tenor saxophone. He emphasizes the root (E) and 5th (B) notes over the I (E) chord in measures 1–4, and in measures 5 and 6 of the IV (A) chord, he rides the root (A) and ♭7th (G) notes to underscore the A7 tonality. Clapton concludes his brief instrumental break by resolving to the root (E) note in measure 7.

Fig. 11

Outro-Guitar Solo

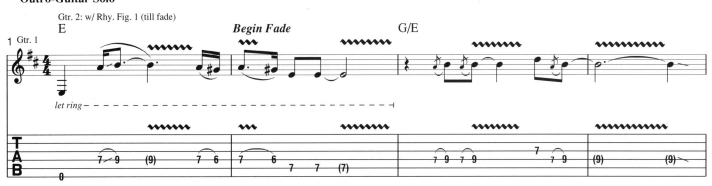

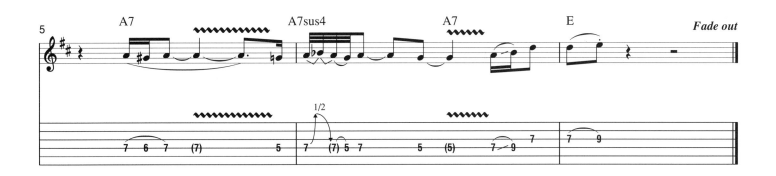

PRIDE AND JOY
(STEVIE RAY VAUGHAN)
Words and Music by Stevie Ray Vaughan

Born in Oak Cliff, Texas (the birthplace of T-Bone Walker) on October 3, 1954, Stevie had the good fortune to have older brother Jimmie guide him on the path to eventual guitar immortality. With help from legendary R&B producer Jerry Wexler, Stevie Ray Vaughan and Double Trouble appeared at the Montreux Jazz festival in 1982. For the next seven years, every recording and live performance only added to his growing reputation. Ironically, just as he was ready to turn his life around following years of substance abuse, he lost it in a horrific helicopter crash on August 27, 1990.

"Pride and Joy" is a spellbinding track not just for Stevie's high-energy, rocking solos, but also his amazing comping, containing walking bass lines and chord forms.

Figure 12—Solo 1

Stevie "kicks out the jams" with relentlessly swinging eighth notes and triplets, in the process "running the changes" with cunning and skill. In measure 4 (I) Stevie shifts to the octave root position of the E basic blues scale, where he bends the ♭7th leading tone (D) one quarter step to the "true blue note" *in between* the ♭7th and major 7th (D♯) combined with the E/B dyad at fret 12. For the V (B) chord in measure 9, he works an open-position broken B7 chord followed by an ear-popping choice of notes for the IV (A) chord in measure 10.

With his second chorus of blues, he continues with the motif of open strings by playing the fretted root (E) along with string 1 (E) open in measure 13 and G/E (5th and ♭7th of A) with string 1 over the IV chord in measures 17 and 18. Some highlights: measure 19, where the hammer-ons, bends, and pull-offs—all phrased as triplets—mark the major 3rd (G♯), ♭7th (D), 5th (B), and root (E) notes of the I chord; and measure 22, with rapid hammers and pulls involving the root (A) notes of the IV chord.

23 Full Band

24 Slow Demo

Fig. 12

Tune down 1/2 step:
(low to high) E♭–A♭–D♭–G♭–B♭–E♭

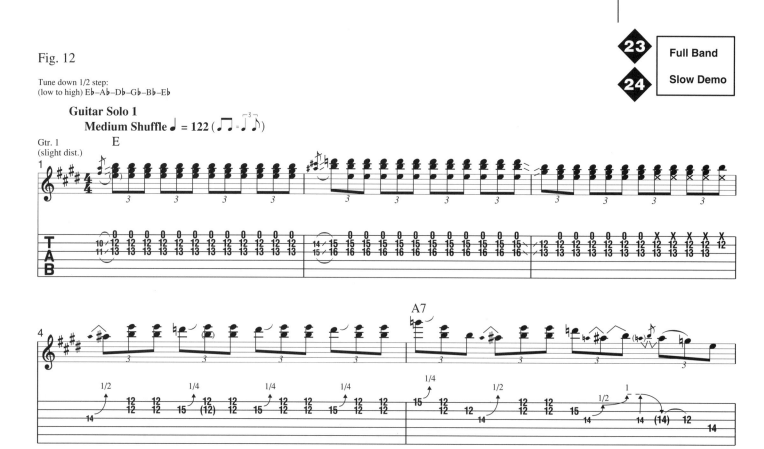

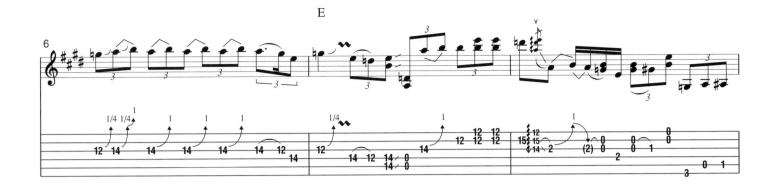

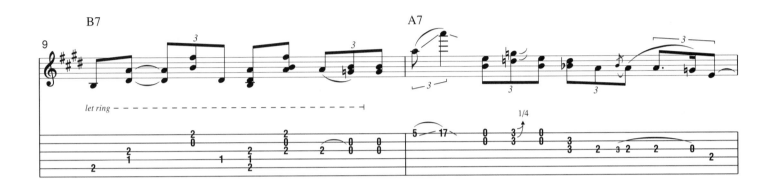

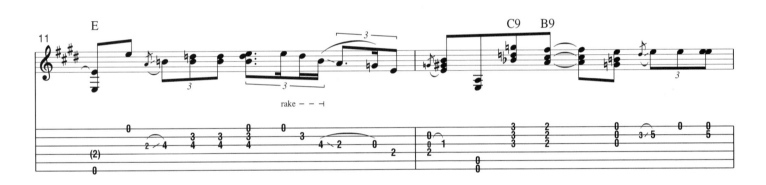

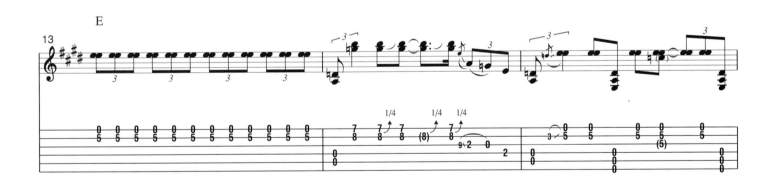

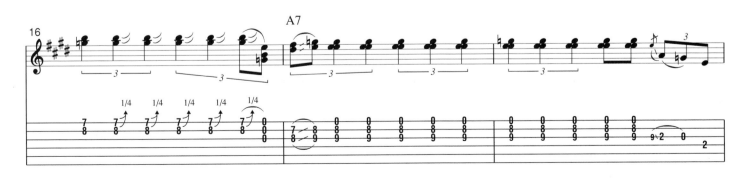

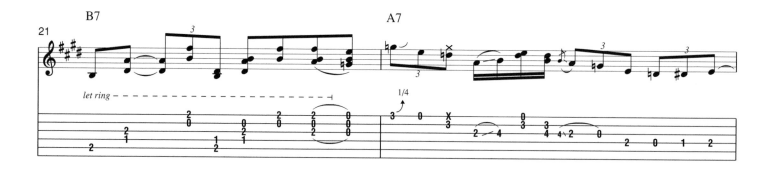

Figure 13—Solo 2

Stevie reprises some of the dyads from solo 1 in measures 3 and 4 of the I (E) chord. He then builds musical anticipation with D/B (5th and ♭7th) and E/C♯ (6th and root) plus string 1 open in measures 1 and 2, respectively, for a powerful ascending sequence as a kickoff to the solo. On a roll, Stevie executes a series of Albert King bends in measure 6 of the IV chord.

A champ at the V (B)–IV (A) cadence in measures 9 and 10 of a 12-bar blues, Stevie subtly suggests the V chord with F♯/B (5th and root) and the IV chord with the D/B (sus4 and 9th) dyad resolved to B/G (♭7th and 9th) on beats 2 and 3.

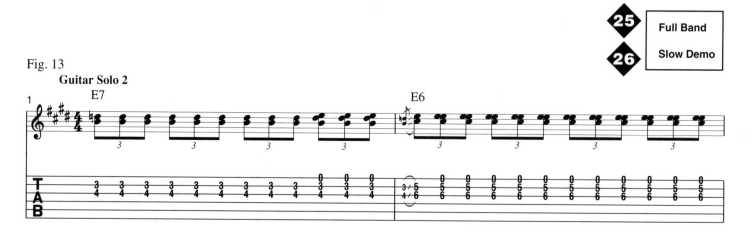

Fig. 13

Guitar Solo 2

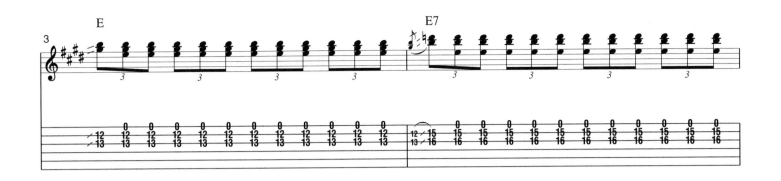

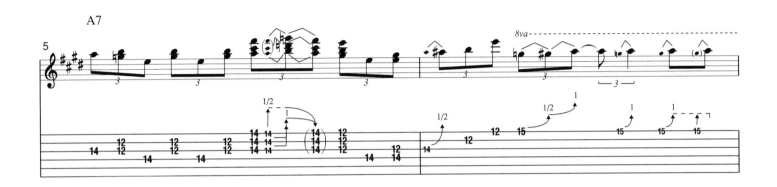

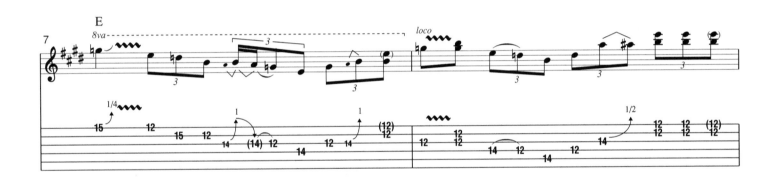

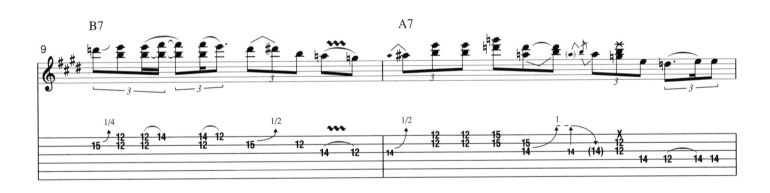

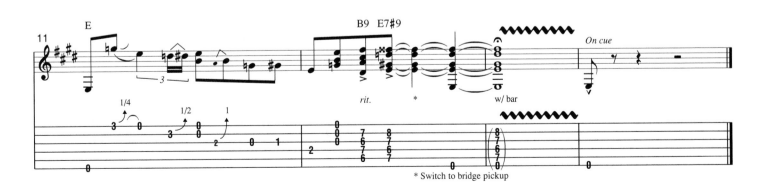

* Switch to bridge pickup

RAMBLIN' MAN
(THE ALLMAN BROTHERS BAND)
Words and Music by Dickey Betts

"Ramblin' Man" is a landmark country-rock classic from 1973, based on diatonic major and minor chords. With two lyrically joyous solos, it is a must-learn for serious twangers. (Note: The recording is actually in G♯, necessitating the use of a capo at fret 1 or tuning up one half step.)

Figure 14—Solo 1

The relative minor scale has always been one of Betts' favorites, and he intelligently applies the E Aeolian (relative to G major) mode at the fifteenth position and the octave root position at fret 12. After firmly establishing the major tonality with a singing bend of the 9th or 2nd (A) from the Aeolian mode to the major 3rd (B), he basically treats measures 1–6 (I and IV) as a G tonality and emphasizes the root (G), 3rd (B), and 5th (D) notes from the G major triad. Measures 11 (vi) and 15 (I) are the only time that Betts uses the ♭6th (C) from the Aeolian mode as a quick pull-off to the B (major 7th of C and 3rd of G) for melodic variety.

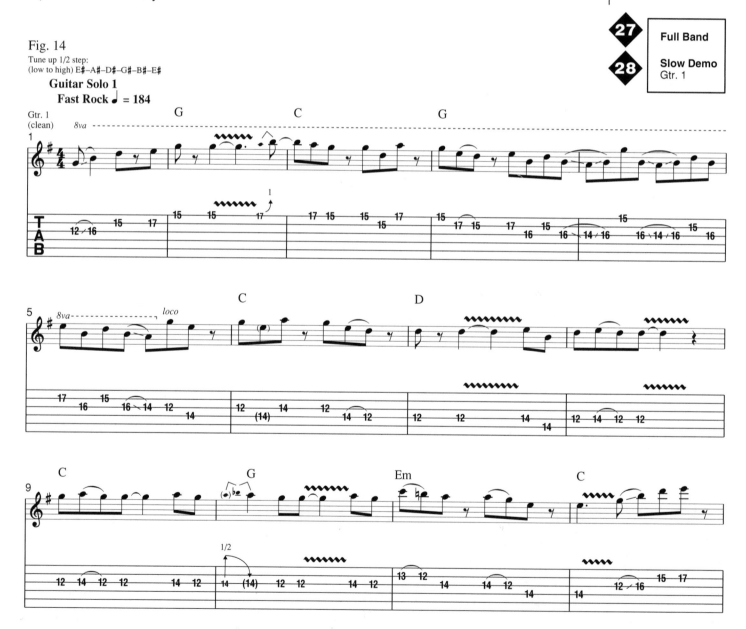

Fig. 14

Tune up 1/2 step:
(low to high) E♯–A♯–D♯–G♯–B♯–E♯

Guitar Solo 1
Fast Rock ♩ = 184

27 Full Band

28 Slow Demo
Gtr. 1

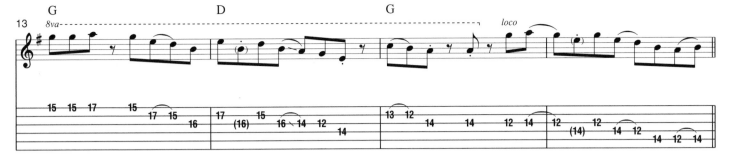

Figure 15—Solo 2 (Outro)

Over a I–♭VII–IV–I (G–F–C–G) four-measure vamp, Betts "rambles" off into the sunset in style. In measures 1–32 (Gtr. 1) he locks into the "B.B. King box" around fret 8 and twirls many variations of the 2nd (A) bent to the melodic 3rd (B) and resolved back to the root. In measures 33–64, Betts overdubs a harmony guitar (Gtr. 2) in thirds for a spectacular sequence that builds to a giddy climax of accelerating and relentlessly loopy bends in measures 57–64. Just when you think you have heard it all, however, Betts eliminates the harmony guitar, whips out his slide (Gtr. 7) in measure 64, and sails on downstream to the fade out.

29 Full Band

30 Slow Demos:
Gtr. 1   meas. 1-39, 49-52, 57-58
Gtr. 7   meas. 64-71

Fig. 15

Outro-Guitar Solo

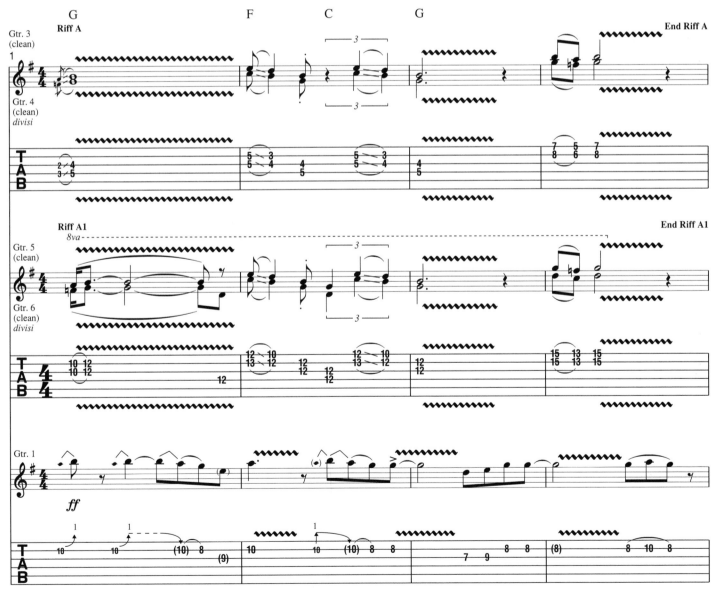

Gtrs. 3 & 4 and 5 & 6: w/ Riffs A & A1 (repeat until fade)

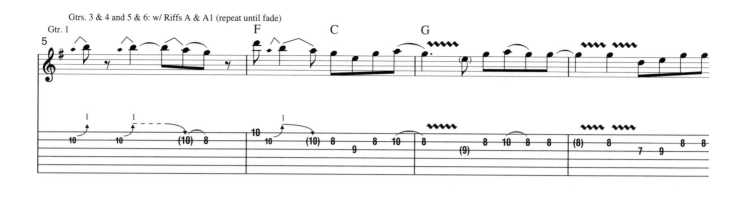

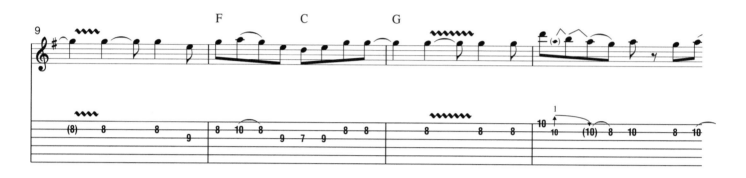

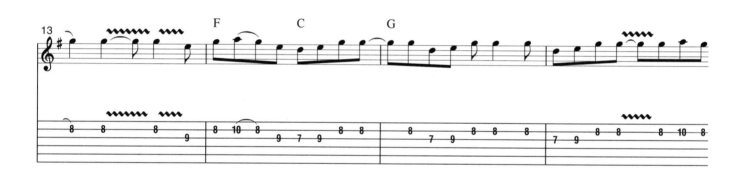

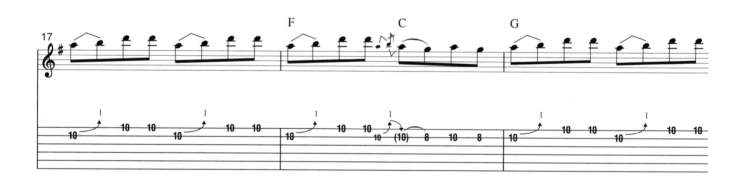

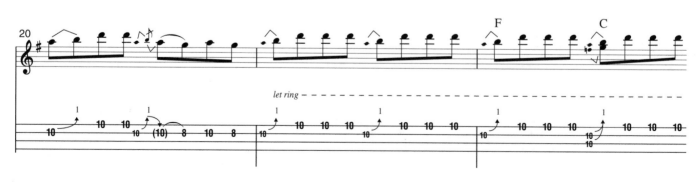

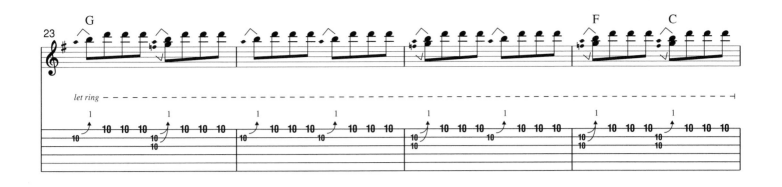

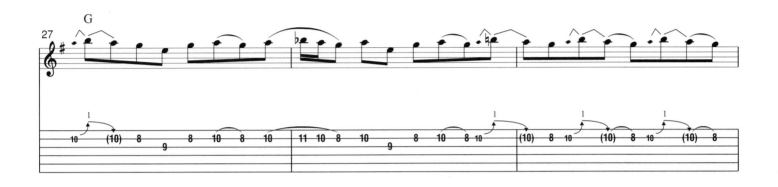

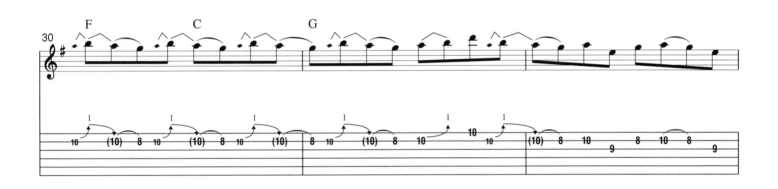

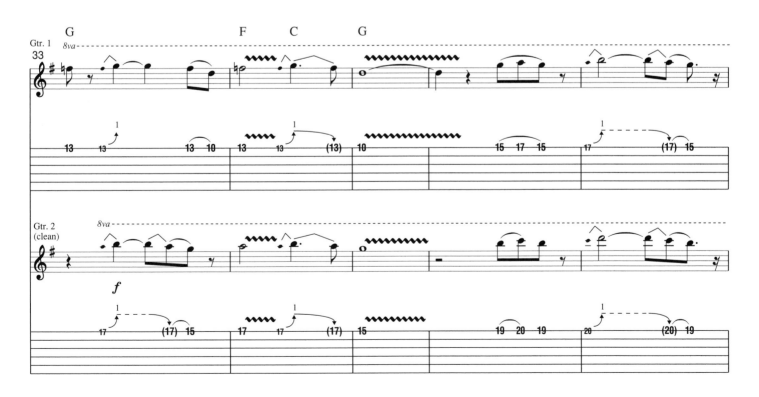

RIDIN' THE STORM OUT
(REO SPEEDWAGON)
Words and Music by Gary Richrath

Named after the fabled (in some circles!) truck and fire engine company, REO Speedwagon formed in 1968 in Champaign, Illinois, with Gary Richrath on lead guitar and Terry Luttrell on lead vocals fronting the group. In 1981, their ship came in when *High Infidelity* and the single "Keep On Loving You" both hit the top of the charts, with the album maintaining the position for fifteen weeks and selling 7 million copies.

The 1973 hit "Ridin' the Storm Out" is an excellent example of dramatic minor-key chords in the service of a defiant lyric and searing, screaming Les Paul/Marshall solos designed to get the lighters in the air. The live version (from *You Get What You Play For*) is examined here.

Figure 16—Solo 1

The sixteen-measure solo flies over vi–V–IV (Am–G–F) changes for twelve measures and vi–vii (Bm)–I (C)–vii chords for the remaining four measures. Richrath (Gtr. 1) adheres to the KISS (keep it simple, stupid) principle by using the A minor pentatonic scale in several positions—except for measures 4 and 14, where he briefly inserts the 2nd (B) and 6th (F♯) from the A Dorian mode.

In measures 6 and 7, Richrath glisses down the neck, restarting his campaign at the fifth position with a run down the scale before jump cutting back to the twentieth position for the piercing bend to the octave root. He maintains his place at the top (literally and figuratively) in measures 9–16 with the octave root position of the A scale at fret 17, from which he draws whippy pull-offs as well as three siren-like, step-and-one-half bends from the ♭7th (G) to the ♭9th (B♭) in measures 13 and 14.

31 Full Band

32 Slow Demo
Gtr. 1

Fig. 16

Guitar Solo 1

Moderately fast Rock ♩ = 142

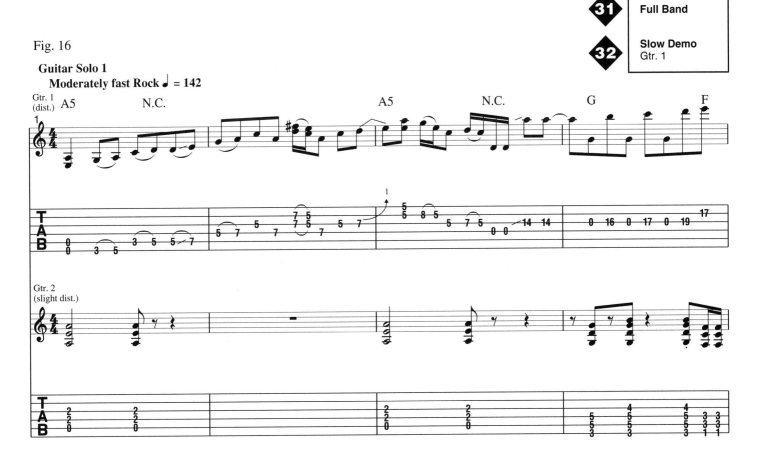

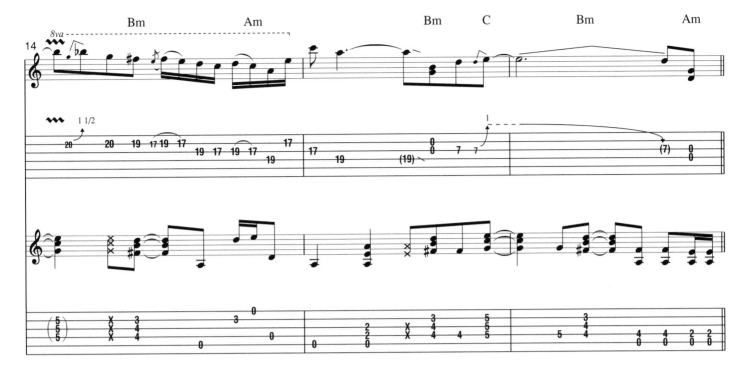

Figure 17—Solo 2

Over the two-measure vamp of vi–vii–I–vii–vi, Richrath starts at the fifth position of the A minor pentatonic scale, arriving at the octave root seventeenth position (where it morphs into the A Dorian mode with the addition of the 2nd and 6th) in measure 7 and cranking almost non-stop through to measure 23. Measures 9–12 are absolutely stunning; Richrath builds amazing forward motion through the manipulation of a handful of scale tones (root, ♭3rd, 5th, and 6th). The one-step bends of the ♭3rd (C) to the 4th (D) in measures 17 and 18 howl with sustain and distortion and contrast with the lightning pull-offs and hammer-ons in measures 19 and 20.

Full Band

Slow Demo:
Gtr. 1 meas. 1-24

Fig. 17

Guitar Solo 2

46

ROCK AND ROLL ALL NITE

(KISS)

Words and Music by Paul Stanley and Gene Simmons

The mega-moneymaking and marketing machine began in 1973 in the Big Apple, when former Wicked Lester bassist Gene Simmons and rhythm guitarist Paul Stanley put "musician wanted" ads in *Rolling Stone* and the *Village Voice*. Drummer Peter Criss and lead guitarist Ace Frehley responded, and the four original members were united. Within two weeks of their first gig they were signed to the new Casablanca label, and their self-titled debut appeared in 1974. A year later, three more albums were in the can, and the band's non-stop touring had sown the seeds for a burgeoning fan base known as the Kiss Army. In 1975 *Alive!* smashed the Top 40, and the live single "Rock and Roll All Nite" partied to #14.

Figure 18

You want an anthem? You got it with "Rock and Roll All Nite" and its cheerfully libidinous message. Measures 1–6 alternate I–V boogie patterns, and Frehley plays typical rock 'n' roll unison bends of a 5th in the root position of the A minor pentatonic scale. Jacking up the intensity quotient in measure 9, he fixes himself at the octave root position at fret 17 through to measure 14. The bend of the 4th (D) to the 5th (E) on string 3, followed by the fretted 5th and root (A) in measure 9, is a blues classic with a pedigree at least as far back as T-Bone Walker. In measures 15 and 16 he repeats the barre chords from measures 7 and 8 before launching into an exceedingly hip (for rock!) series of double stops and trills in measure 17.

35 Full Band

36 Slow Demo
Gtr. 1

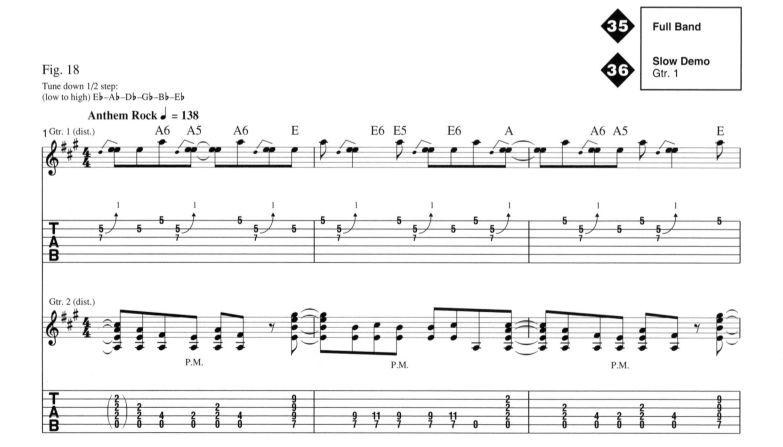

Fig. 18

Tune down 1/2 step:
(low to high) Eb–Ab–Db–Gb–Bb–Eb

Anthem Rock ♩ = 138

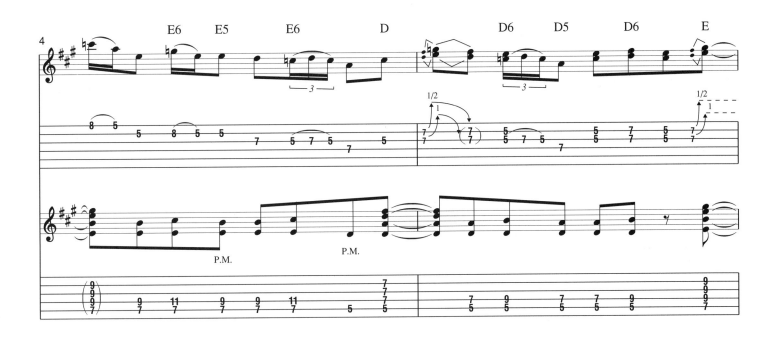

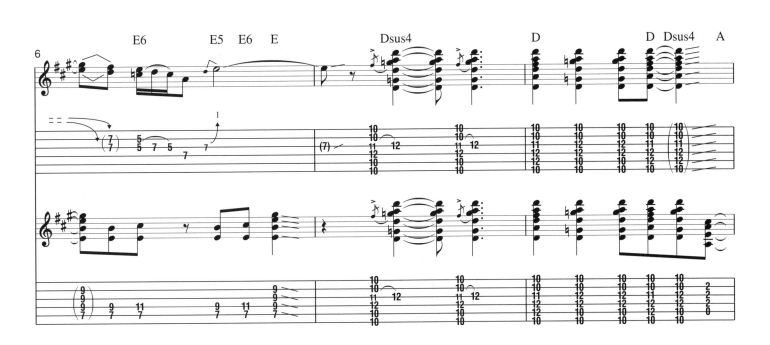

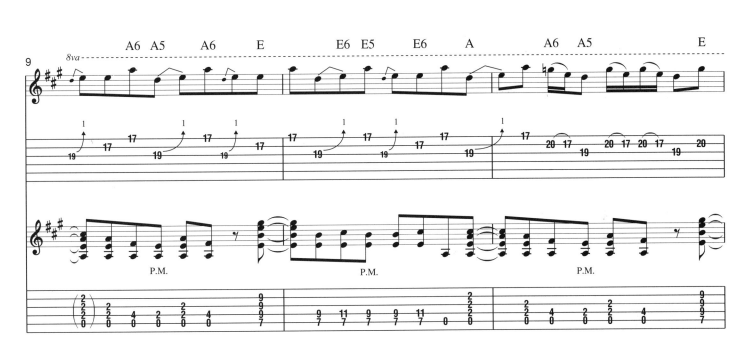

ROCK AND ROLL HOOCHIE KOO

(RICK DERRINGER)

Words and Music by Rick Derringer

The title says it all: rock 'n' roll and the blues (courtesy of the allusion to Muddy Waters' "Hoochie Coochie Man") in the service of a tune about young lust. Without pretense, Derringer plays hard and fast on this 1973 opus.

Figure 19

The sixteen-measure progression under the solo is built on a one-measure riff of A5–C5–D5–C5 similar to the vocal verses. In measures 1–8, Derringer (Gtr. 1) rips and runs in the octave root position of the A minor pentatonic scale at fret 17. Authentic, traditional blues licks are scattered about like confetti, including the bending of the 4th (D) to the 5th (E) on string 3 while holding the ♭7th (G) on string 2 to form the interval of a 3rd in measures 1 and 3.

In measures 9–11 he drops dynamically to the open position of the A scale, then works the root position at fret 5 with snappy little descending blues phrases with roots that go back to T-Bone Walker. Notice how he repeats the blues riff from measures 1 and 3 in measure 10, albeit an octave lower, as a motif. Continuing to use dynamics of register to his advantage, he executes a series of ascending, Hendrix-like unison bends in measures 12 and 13 and then abruptly glisses back down to the root position of the scale. From there, he begins another ascending run that eventually peaks out at the tenth position and the 4th (D) in measure 15. Capping his solo in measure 16, he reverses direction, ending up in the root position at fret 5 on the 5th (E). It ain't profound, but it sure fits this seventies classic.

37 Full Band

38 Slow Demo
Gtr. 1

Fig. 19

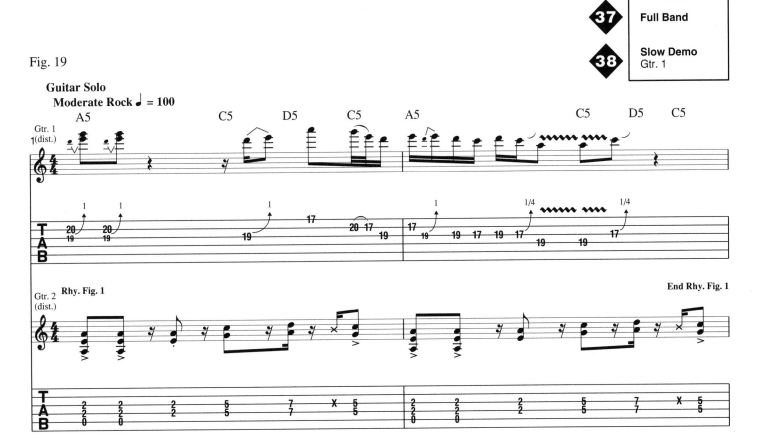

ROCK AROUND THE CLOCK
(BILL HALEY AND HIS COMETS)
Words and music by Max C. Freedman and Jimmy DeKnight

Danny Cedrone (born June 20, 1920 in Jamesville, New York and died June 17, 1954 in Philadelphia), a true "unsung hero" of rock 'n' roll, played the chops-challenging solo on the original recording. He had previously played the same solo (which had been inspired by Les Paul and his version of "How High the Moon") on "Rock This Joint," and perhaps recognizing the similarity between the two tunes, opted to reproduce it.

Figure 20

Cedrone's 12-bar solo is brilliantly composed and is worth sussing out measure by measure. Dig that virtually the entire production is in the root position of the A composite scale, with copious passing and chromatic tones.

Measure 1–4 (I): Cedrone peals off dizzy sixteenth notes containing the 2nd (open B-string), 5th (E), 6th (F♯), and ♭7th (G).

Measures 5 and 6 (IV): The vertical motion of the bluesy half-step bend of the 9th (B) to the ♭3rd (C) contrasts dynamically with the linear torrent in measures 1–4. The inclusion of the 5th (A) and 3rd (F♯) of D nails the IV tonality.

Measures 7 and 8 (I): Cedrone slows up a bit and shows his swing chops with a classic hammer-on from the ♭3rd (C) to the major 3rd followed by the 5th (E) in measure 7.

Measures 9 and 10 (V): If you thought measures 1–4 were fearful, check out this "bad boy" run. In measure 9 Cedrone descends chromatically like a roller coaster from the 5th (B) down to the root (E). Without missing (or skipping) a beat, he continues descending (scale-wise, but not chromatically) from the root in measure 10 to the ♭7th (D), 6th (C♯), 5th, and 3rd (G♯) with resolution to the low root on the downbeat of beat 3.

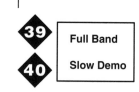

Fig. 20

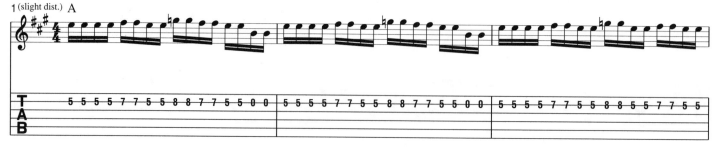

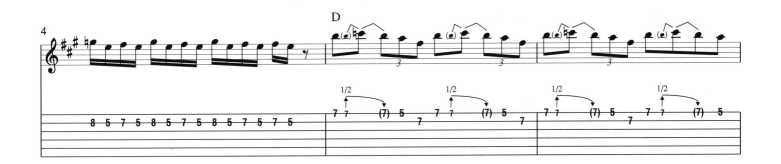

SMOKE ON THE WATER
(DEEP PURPLE)

**Words and Music by Ritchie Blackmore, Ian Gillian,
Roger Glover, Jon Lord and Ian Paice**

Richard Blackmore was born in Somerset, England on April 14, 1945 and is a founding father of heavy metal, while also having an appealing blue streak. His work with DP and Rainbow shows a fine ear for melody with Strat-cracking chops.

Figure 21

The twenty-six-measure solo break only contains I (G5), IV (C5), and ♭VII (F5) chords, but the arrangement is quite clever, building to a dramatic climax that allows Blackmore to take advantage of his scale knowledge and bluesy phrasing for maximum impact.

Blackmore (Gtr. 2) employs the E minor scale in measures 1–4. In measures 5–8 he continues following the changes with similar note choices. However, he creates hip tension in measure 5 (I) by bending one, one half, and then one step from the ♭7th (F) to the root (G), major 7th (F♯), and root, respectively. In measure 7 (IV) he shows real class by changing scales (and keys) to the root position of the C Dorian mode (with the addition of the ♭5th—G♭ on beat 2) at fret 8, as a C5 allows wide latitude in terms of major and minor scales. In dynamic contrast, Blackmore riffs like mad in the root position of the G blues scale over the IV chord in measure 11 and closes the increment with a very cool, time-altering *quarter*-note triplet with the 4th (C) bent to the 5th (D) in measure 12.

Measures 13–16 move from the root position of the G blues scale up through the 10th position, with another stop at the root position of the C Dorian mode over the IV chord (measure 15). The ♭VII (F) chord in measure 19 is suggested with expanded tonality by the 6th (D), root (F), and 5th (C) notes from the root position of the G Aeolian mode. Blackmore ends his brilliant sojourn on "Lake Geneva" with the ♭7th (F) bent to the root (G) and then released, vibratoed, and sustained for six beats into measure 24 (implying a bluesy dominant tonality). "Smoke" on the fingerboard!

Fig. 21

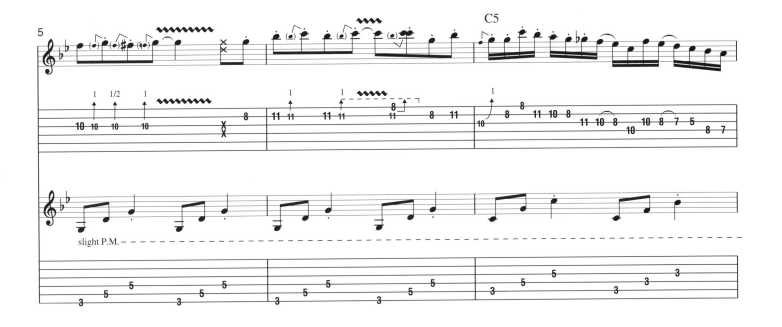

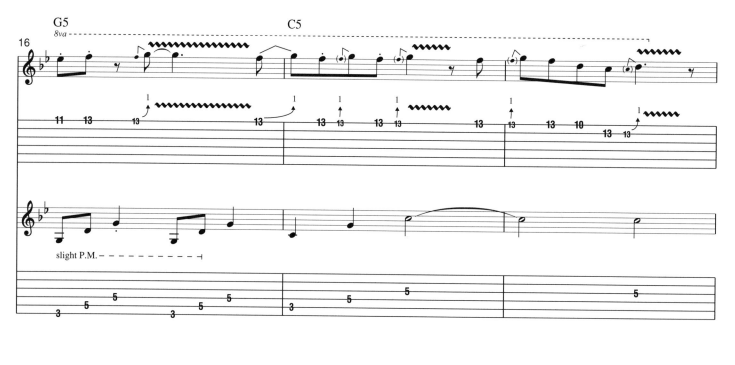

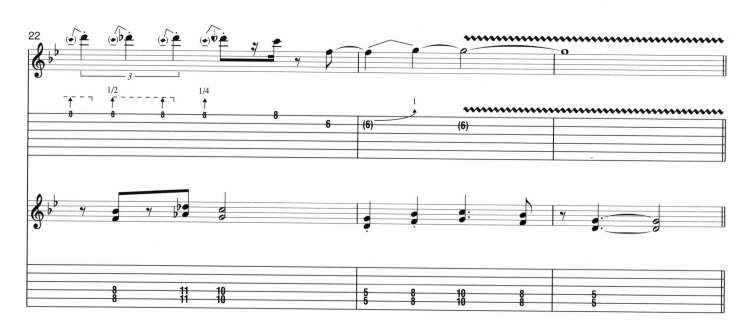

SWEET EMOTION
(AEROSMITH)
Words and Music by Steven Tyler and Tom Hamilton

Joseph Perry was born in Boston on September 10, 1950, and has developed a muscular yet funky style based on the blues via the Bluesbreakers and his hero Jeff Beck circa his stint with the Yardbirds. Along with his image of playing "Keith Richards" to Tyler's "Mick Jagger," his playing has influenced a generation of aspiring string twisters.

Figure 22

Perry pops and burns over a two-measure "E" vamp for twenty-one measures until the fadeout. Measures 1–4 find Perry kicking his solo into gear with an aggressively attacked dyad at the 16th position on strings 1 and 2. Consisting of G#/D, it is the ♭7th and major 3rd from a common E7 voicing beloved to blues cats from back in the Delta all the way up to the present. In measure 7, he nails the E major tonality on beat 2 with a hammer-on from the ♭3rd (G) to the major 3rd (G♯) followed by the root.

Perry makes a dramatic change of register in measures 9 and 10, when he drops dynamically to the open root position and plays some darn good country-blues licks. The one-step bend of the 2nd (F♯) to the major 3rd (G♯) that resolves to the root (open high E string), along with the 6th (C♯) bent one step to the jazzy major 7th (D♯) and resolving to the 5th (open B string) in measure 10, also sound like they belong on somebody's back porch down South. From measures 11 to 21, though, he just plain wears out his B string with relentless bends in varying pitches from the 6th and ♭7th (D), goosed by undulating vibrato to keep the energy level peaking like a VU meter on overload.

Fig. 22

43 Full Band

44 Slow Demo
Gtr. 1 meas. 1-22

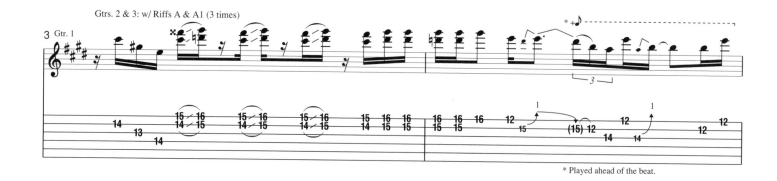

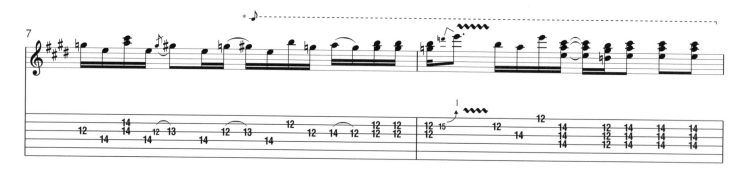

* Played ahead of the beat.

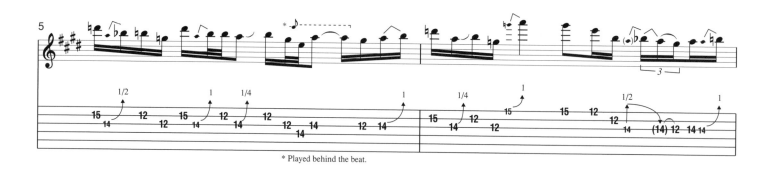

* Played behind the beat.

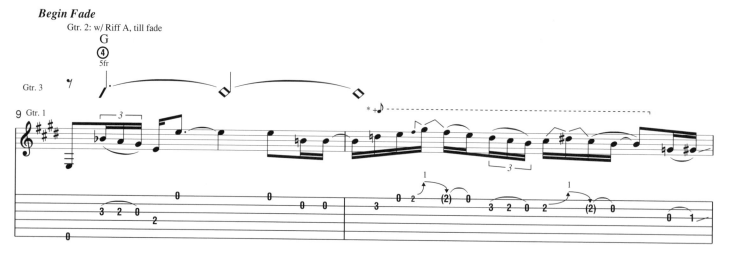

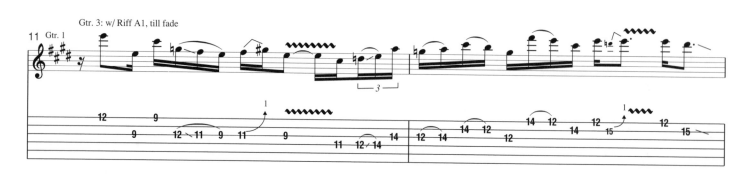

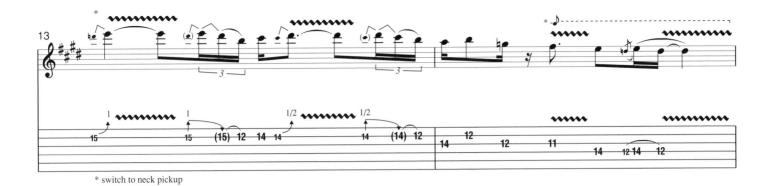

* switch to neck pickup

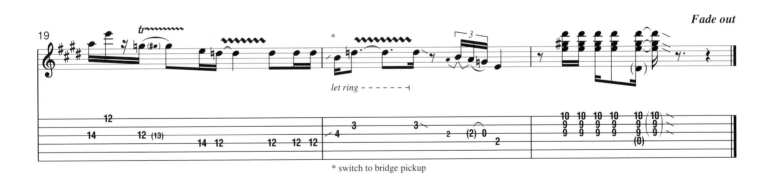

* switch to bridge pickup

WHITE ROOM
(CREAM)
Words and Music by Jack Bruce and Pete Brown

"White Room" appeared on the monster 2-disk set, *Wheels of Fire*, in that banner year for counterculture rock, 1968. The album snared the coveted #1 spot in August, sharing the Top 10 with the Doors' *Waiting for the Sun*, Hendrix' *Are You Experienced?*, and Cream's previous release, *Disraeli Gears*, while the single rose to #6. Besides his ambiguous relationship to the blues, Clapton has also wrestled with his gargantuan fame and its effect on his music. Be that as it may, at this point with Cream he seems to have been happy with his big rock-star status, flaunting his improvisational brilliance, and we are all the richer for it.

Figure 23—Outro Solo

Clapton legitimized the wah-wah pedal for rock musicians with his aggressive footwork on "White Room," though Jimi Hendrix likely messed with it first. As would be expected, blues licks abound in the grinding, twenty-six-measure outro solo. Due to the modal nature of the chord sequence, Clapton must be responsible for creating the requisite tension and release. In measures 1–6 he finesses the top three strings (and string 4 for the resolution to the root, D) with repeated, tension-inducing bends of the 4th (G) to the 5th (A) along with the peppery, sensually-vibratoed, bluesy ♭3rd (F).

Starting in measure 9, Clapton continues with tightly focused root-position licks on the middle strings that repeatedly resolve to the root note. In measure 12, he climbs up to the top strings for dynamic contrast while repeating pull-offs from the ♭7th (C) to the 5th (A) into measure 13. The bluesy C/A (♭7th and 5th) dyad in measures 17–18 adds texture and harmony, while repetition of the root in measure 19, ending with sustain and vibrato, relaxes the tension briefly—only to be pumped up again with zingy pull-offs from the 4th (G) to the ♭3rd (F) and the root to the ♭7th (C) in measure 20.

Performance tip: Generally speaking, Clapton rocks the wah-wah rhythmically on the downbeat of each quarter note almost non-stop through out the solo.

Fig. 23

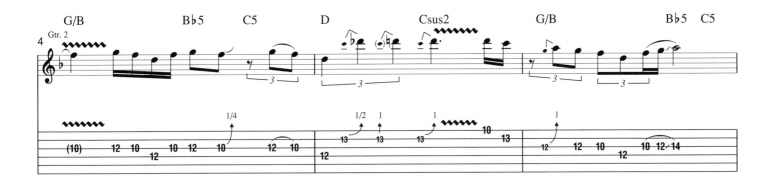

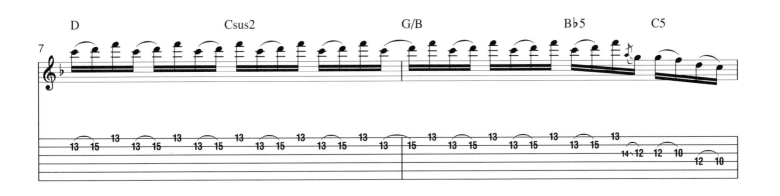

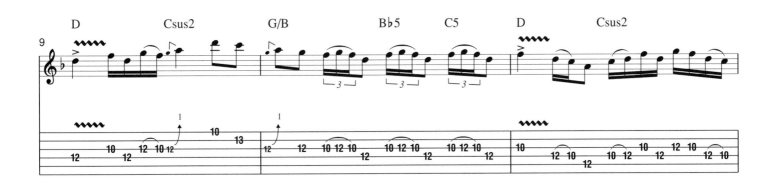

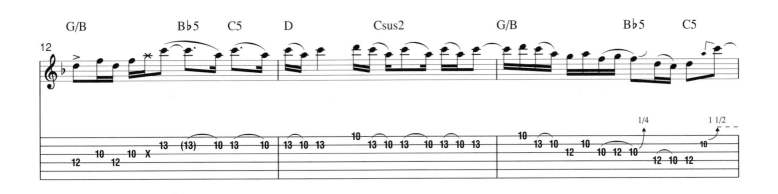

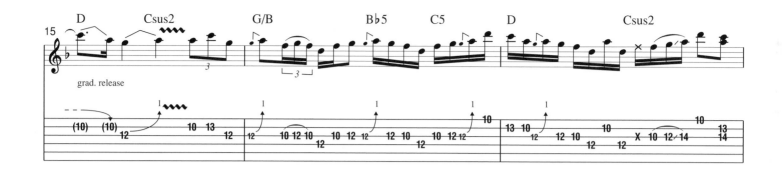

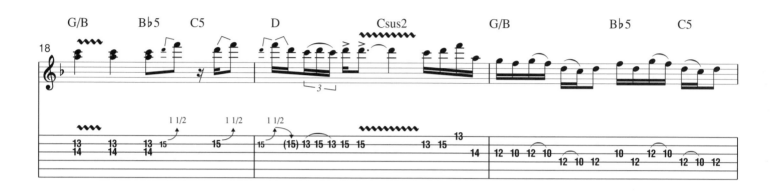

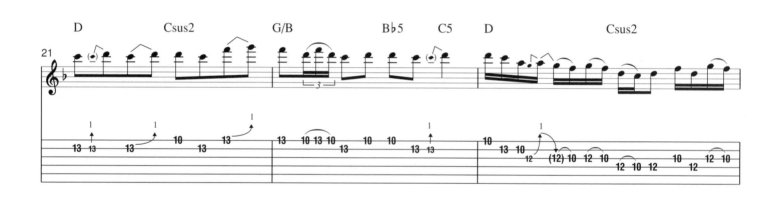

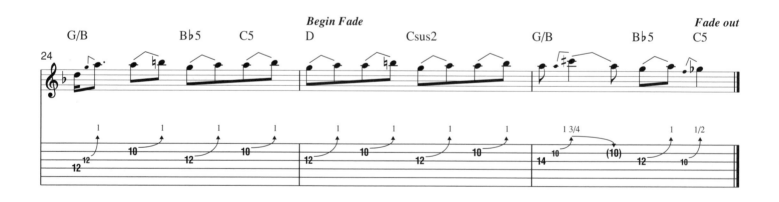